SPACE CAMP®

The Great Adventure for NASA Hopefuls

ANNE BAIRD

PHOTOGRAPHS BY
ROBERT KOROPP

FOREWORD BY
Rear Admiral USN, Ret.,
Alan B. Shepard, Jr.

INTRODUCTION BY
Edward O. Buckbee
Director, U.S. Space & Rocket Center; Founder, U.S. Space Camp

MORROW JUNIOR BOOKS · NEW YORK

To dreamers of all ages,
who won't believe it can't be done.

ACKNOWLEDGMENTS

There are many people we would like to thank for making this book possible: first, Edward O. Buckbee, Director of the U.S. Space & Rocket Center, whose enthusiasm and support for the project made it all happen; also, Lee Sentell, Director of Marketing, whose assistance was invaluable. Rear Admiral USN, Ret., Alan B. Shepard, Jr., has our thanks for his foreword and words of encouragement to young people seeking careers in space; and Karen Sirianno, Program Manager of U.S. Space Camp, our gratitude for her help as technical consultant.

All members of the Space Camp staff endeared themselves to us by their courtesy and cooperation. Thomas J. Burby, Debbie Coulter, Linda Burroughs, Lamar Higgins, Walter R. Chambliss, Fred McDaniel, and Walter Brannon are among those who deserve mention for their extra efforts on our behalf. Counselors Lisa Vest and Jay Osowiecki, leaders of the Wyle team, were outstanding. Above all, we thank the wonderful children and parents of the Wyle team for allowing us to follow their group through Space Camp.

A warm thank-you to William A. Breukelman, Chairman of Imax Corporation; Rose Duignam of Industrial Light & Magic; and NASA for their help in providing us with special photographs. Peri A. Widener, Sharon Denver, and Adam Burkey of Boeing's space station were very helpful. Stanley A. Wainer, Chairman of Wyle Laboratories, generously donated the Wyle team's flight suits to them, and Raymond J. Raff gave us the idea for the book. Thanks to Faith Hamlin, agent, for helping us put the book package together, and Andrea Curley, editor, who guided us with infinite patience and care through the process of creating the book.

No list of acknowledgments would be complete without thanking Joe Baird, whose encouragement and belief in our project was much appreciated. A special thank-you to Phyllis Koropp, who, in addition to supporting us, assisted in the photography and post-production of the book.

PHOTO CREDITS

Permission to use the following photographs is gratefully acknowledged: NASA, pages 3, 32–33 (insert), 36 (insert); U.S. Space Camp/Bob Gathany, page 4.

Space Camp Mission Script © 1991 Alabama Space Science Exhibit Commission. Reproduced with permission.

The names SPACE CAMP, SPACE ACADEMY, AVIATION CHALLENGE, and SPACEDOME THEATER are registered trademarks. © 1991 Alabama Space Science Exhibit Commission.

IMAX® and OMNIMAX® are registered trademarks of Imax Corporation.

Text copyright © 1992 by Anne Baird
Illustrations copyright © 1992 by Robert Koropp

DESIGN BY LOGO STUDIOS / B. GOLD
Printed in Singapore at Tien Wah Press.
1 2 3 4 5 6 7 8 9 10

Library of Congress Cataloging-in-Publication Data
Baird, Anne.
    Space Camp : the great adventure for NASA hopefuls Anne Baird ; photographs by Robert Koropp ; foreword by Rear Admiral USN, Ret., Alan B. Shepard, Jr.; introduction by Edward O. Buckbee.
        p.   cm.
    Summary: Text and photographs follow young campers as they experience NASA-style astronaut training at the U.S. Space Camp in Huntsville, Alabama.
    ISBN 0-688-10227-1 (trade). — ISBN 0-688-10228-X (lib. bdg.)
    1. Astronautics—Juvenile literature. [1. Astronautics. 2. Camps.] I. Koropp, Robert, ill.   II. Title.
TL793.B225   1992
629.45—dc20   91-21587   CIP   AC

FOREWORD

When the other Mercury astronauts and I were selected to be the first Americans in space, there was no tried-and-true method of teaching people what to expect during space travel. They picked us because we were test pilots and used to assignments involving the research and development of new aircraft. We also understood the risks of exploring new frontiers in aviation. I became the first American to fly in space thirty years ago, and I later commanded a mission atop a *Saturn V* rocket and walked

on the moon as an Apollo astronaut. The missions went much as anticipated because the astronauts and engineers were all professionals who understood the challenges and achieved their goals.

Thirty years is less than the blink of an eye in terms of human history, but the space program has triggered entire new fields of discovery in technology that have improved the quality of life for people all over the civilized world. I am excited about the youngsters of today and the abundance of opportunities for them to be associated with the space program and other technical fields. The boys and girls now in school will grow into adults whose contributions to the betterment of all humankind could easily eclipse what has happened in the past three decades. I have learned a great deal about today's young men and women through my close personal association with the U.S. Space Camp. I enjoy my many trips to meet and talk with the trainees and hear of their aspirations for the future.

It is difficult to appreciate what a great program this is without actually walking through the doors and seeing the youngsters in action. I urge families interested in the space program to visit the U.S. Space & Rocket Center in Alabama or the U.S. Astronaut Hall of Fame in Florida for a preview of Space Camp trainees in action. This book is a perfect introduction to Space Camp. It beautifully captures the excitement and drama of youngsters living a remarkable adventure in space without actually having to leave the ground.

To the young people who will be the astronauts, scientists, engineers, and leaders of the twenty-first century, I encourage you to eagerly accept the challenge of math and science courses in school because there are still new frontiers for your generation to explore.

REAR ADMIRAL ALAN B. SHEPARD, JR.
U.S. Navy (Retired)
President, Mercury Seven Foundation

INTRODUCTION

Astronauts who visit the U.S. Space Camp bring backgrounds and stories of flights ranging from 15-minute suborbital missions to three months in the Skylab space station. But they leave with essentially the same thing: a sincere respect for the caliber of the young people growing up today and a sense that the future is in good hands.

Many young men and women, eager to get a head start on their futures, are signing up for as many math and science classes as possible while striving for excellence in everything they do.

These characteristics typify the trainees we see at Space Camp. Whether they are fourth graders learning Newton's laws of motion or seniors breezing through systems procedures in the gung-ho Aviation Challenge program, they clearly envision themselves on the front line of achievement in the twenty-first century. They may become astronauts, computer engineers, scientists, or educators; they may even enter professions that we can't yet anticipate.

When we designed the first Space Camp program a decade ago, we hoped to attract the kind of youngster who would be challenged by our exercises in decision making, teamwork, and leadership. Knowing that some of our early graduates are now in military academies and striving to become astronauts, we rejoice in our contributions to these young people.

Space Camp's present challenge is to attract and motivate the next class of young people to say, "We can't wait to get started."

The book *Space Camp* will encourage these adventurers. Anne Baird's energizing text and Robert Koropp's dramatic photographs perfectly capture the diversity, excitement, and challenge that is the Space Camp experience, and will inspire all those who want to make the universe that is space their own.

EDWARD O. BUCKBEE
Director, U.S. Space & Rocket Center
Founder, U.S. Space Camp

CONTENTS

DAY ONE
Orientation and Rocket History

"I've never seen anything like it," says a girl from Iowa. "It looks like it's ready to go into orbit!"

She steps off the Space Camp bus and stands in front of Space Camp's Habitat, staring at the building where she and eight hundred other campers will live and work during the coming week. It's something to stare at.

Habitat is huge and high-tech. Built to look like NASA's proposed space station, it has six enormous horizontal metal tubes that project from the four-story towers of the central structure. The tubes, which are divided into sleep stations for older campers, are windowless, except for the domed portholes on their ends. These windows stare out over the Space and Rocket Center, where Space Camp is housed, like the electronic eyes of a passing spaceship.

"Well, it's not *supposed* to be like home," says Jonathan Brooks, a twelve-year-old from Texas.

He can't wait to check it out. He dreams of becoming an astronaut. The question is, *How*? What does he have to do to become one?

Jonathan has come to Space Camp to find the answers. Already he feels he's come to the right place. Hundreds of children are pouring into the camp today. Like him, they've come to spend a week training in the most famous space camp in the world.

Space Camp was started in Huntsville, Alabama, in 1982 by its director, Edward O. Buckbee. It had only 850 trainees that first year. Buckbee was inspired by the famous rocket scientist Dr. Wernher von Braun, who believed children would love a camp where they could experience NASA-style astronaut training. Von Braun was right! His idea caught on like wildfire. And it spread.

By 1990, twenty-five thousand children, teenagers, and adults from almost every nation in the world, including the Soviet Union, had attended either the first Space Camp in Alabama or the new one at the Kennedy Space Center in Florida. Others have recently opened in Japan and Europe.

Jonathan looks around for the girl from Iowa. She's way ahead of him already, chatting and laughing with another girl from the bus. Time for him to move on, too. He picks up his bag and heads through Habitat's doors.

Inside, it's a whole new world! A dummy astronaut hangs suspended from the ceiling. Everyday things have different names in "NASA speak," the technical language astronauts use. The porthole-shaped windows are labeled "Earth Study"; water fountains, "H_2O Dispensers"; bathrooms, "Waste Management."

Each sleeping bay is named after either a planet, a constellation, or a business sponsor of Space Camp. Names such as "Venus," "Orion," or "Martin Marietta" are painted over the doors.

Friendly counselors help Jonathan register in the large, open central hall. He is given his ID tag and learns he is on Wyle team, and assigned to Orion sleeping bay in the younger campers' dorm rooms in Habitat. He is fitted for his flight suit and lines up at the Interplanetary Bank to exchange his cash for "shuttle bucks," the legal tender of Space Camp.

Next, Jonathan rushes downstairs to stash his gear in his locker and make up his bunk. He meets three other boys from Wyle in his dorm room: Jonathan Anderson and Reed Barrickman, from Georgia, and Eric Harrison, from Mississippi. The nervousness he felt about not knowing anyone starts to fade. Everyone's new to Space Camp!

The loudspeaker booms: "All Space Campers upstairs to the Team Room!"

The Team Room is large enough to hold all the Space Campers and their counselors. Assemblies are held and projects are built there. Small groups meet wherever there is a quiet space to sit down together.

A staff member begins their first meeting on this Sunday afternoon by leading a lively question-and-answer game about space: "What does the word 'astronaut' mean?" "Star traveler!" "Which three planets are surrounded by rings?" "Saturn, Uranus, and Jupiter!"

Next, camp rules and counselors are introduced to the trainees. Jonathan Brooks and his new friends meet their day counselor, a teacher named Lisa Vest. Jay Osowiecki, a future airline pilot, is their night counselor.

Lisa leads her twelve campers outside under the trees to get acquainted with them. She asks them about themselves and about why they came to Space Camp. When things have quieted down, she takes them back to the Team Room, where she distributes the Astronaut Log Books. This is where they'll record everything they learn and see—just like real astronauts do. Their red team visors and team T-shirts are passed out. They'll wear these special clothes every day.

Jonathan pulls on his Space Camp T-shirt with the bold shuttle logo on the front and "Wyle Laboratories" printed across the back. He is excited. Already he feels different.

Lisa tells them, "You're the Wyle team now. Everything you do matters. You'll learn as a team, work as a team, play as a team. If one of you goofs off, you hurt your teammates. You'll have to work together!"

The team returns to the central hall, where they first registered. Along the wall there are computer banks, worktables, and informal meeting areas. The children begin to explore their log books and the computer programs they'll use for their daily lessons in space history and

technology. Jena Cataldi, from New Jersey, examines a diagram of the proposed space station in her log book. Cory Ryan, from Ohio, starts up the computer program about NASA's space shuttle. With Lisa's help, the rest of the team load the same program on their computers and are soon learning about the shuttle.

They learn that the shuttle's main job is to transport astronauts and scientific equipment between Earth and space. They find that the shuttle has four main parts: the airplane-like orbiter that carries the crew and their equipment and experiments to space and back; the solid rocket boosters that give the shuttle immediate power for lift-off; the external tank; and the main engines. The external tank holds liquid propellant for the main engines to use during launch and ascent.

Each space shuttle, Lisa tells them, has a mission, or a set of jobs and experiments the crew performs, which are designed to help us learn more about space. An important goal of every mission is to discover how to make it easier and safer for people to travel, live, and work away from Earth.

"Okay, Wyle," says Lisa, settling her group on the floor by a window. "We've learned a little about NASA's shuttle and about shuttle missions. It's time to talk about your Space Camp Shuttle Mission! You'll be doing it in four days. I bet you'd like to know what crew assignments you'll have on Mission Day."

"Yes! All right!"

Jonathan and his teammates lean forward eagerly. Mission Day is the most important day at Space Camp! On Thursday they'll fly a simulated mission in a mock-up of the first space shuttle, *Columbia*. They'll be using equipment just like NASA's, following a Space Camp Mission Script. It sounds great! But how are they going to get ready?

Lisa explains that the camp program will teach them what they need to know. After they learn about the different jobs on a shuttle mission, each camper will write down three jobs he or she would like to perform.

The counselors decide what mission assignments campers get. Their choices are based on what each child prefers; the score he or she earns on a short, simple quiz; and the trainee's special skills and interests.

After the campers receive their crew assignments, they will see copies of the mission script. This tells each crew member exactly what to do and say during the one-hour mission.

Although Space Camp wrote this script, it is based on things that actually happen during a NASA mission—what real astronauts say and do on a shuttle flight.

The campers will also begin hands-on training with the equipment they'll use during their mission. Lisa assures them that if they listen, and work well all week, there's no way they won't be ready!

Jonathan lets out a sigh of relief. "Okay. Tell us about the jobs," he says.

Lisa smiles. "The team will be divided into two six-member crews: Mission Control and Flight Crew. All jobs can be held by either a boy or a girl. And every job is important."

She explains what the Mission Control crew does. The members work at a bank of monitor screens and computers that track every move of the shuttle. Like NASA's Mission Control in Houston, their job is to guide the astronauts through their mission and to help them get home safely. While the Mission Control crew will not be going into space, Lisa reminds the children that each of the jobs is important and interesting. The shuttle wouldn't be able to do its mission without the help of these ground-based specialists. The Mission Control team is led by the flight director.

Jonathan Anderson's ears prick up. He's someone who likes a big job. Flight director sounds good to him.

Lisa lists the other positions on Mission Control. Three of the team members will help guide the shuttle's flight. The tracking officer follows the shuttle's position and course; the launch and landing director assists in its takeoff and return; and the orbiter systems director makes sure that all electrical systems on board are working. Two other trainees will work with the Flight Crew's scientists. The mission scientist monitors the information gathered from mission experiments, while the principal investigator makes certain that they are finished on time. The campers write the jobs down, amazed by the variety of choices they have.

"What about the Flight Crew?" asks Jonathan Brooks, who wants to fly more than anything else in the world.

He knows that the Flight Crew flies the mission, working inside the orbiter. The flight commander heads up the crew. Jonathan would sure like that assignment. He's told Lisa so already. But wanting it doesn't mean he'll get it. Other people may want to be commander, too.

"Well, you know about commander," Lisa says, smiling at him. She explains that position more clearly to everyone else. "The commander sits in the cockpit with the pilot, like the captain of a commercial airplane. He or she is responsible for controlling the shuttle during launch and reentry, and for making final decisions about everything during the flight."

"Right!" Jonathan's face is shining. "It's a great job!"

"A *responsible* job," Lisa reminds him.

Jessica Pfeltz, from Maryland, has a favorite uncle in the Air Force. "What does the pilot do?" she asks.

"He or she helps fly the shuttle. In case anything happens to the commander, the pilot has to be able to fly and land the orbiter safely."

"Wow!" says Jessica.

Lisa adds that the Flight Crew will include four scientists as well. Payload specialists do scientific experiments inside the orbiter. Two mission specialists perform jobs outside their spacecraft—called extravehicular activities, or EVAs—while it is in orbit.

Lisa grins at her excited team. "A Space Camp mission is different from NASA's, of course. A NASA shuttle flight may last as long as ten days. Yours is packed into sixty minutes. And you'll never leave the Training Floor. You'll be back in time for lunch! But you'll have a space adventure you'll never forget. It's the closest you can get on Earth to feeling like a real astronaut!"

"Let's *do* it!" shouts Jonathan. "I can't wait to get started!"

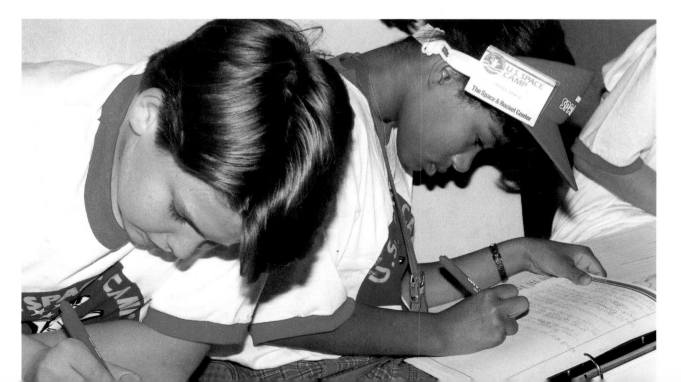

The youngsters now take the quiz that will help determine their assignments. The questions are based on what they've learned so far, showing how carefully they've listened.

Jonathan gets one of the highest scores on the test. That, plus his enthusiasm and desire for a tough Flight Crew assignment, earns him the job he wants: commander.

"Great!" he yells.

High-scoring Jessica will be pilot. She can't wait to call her uncle! Nikki Rankin from Alabama, and Eric Harrison will be mission specialists I and II. Their exuberance and love of action have already marked them as natural space walkers. Redheaded John Kowaleski, from Colorado, and Cory Ryan, both excellent science students, will be payload specialists.

On Mission Control, another bright leader, Jonathan Anderson, is given one of his choices. He'll be the strong anchor to Earth for his team: flight director.

After each of the campers receives an assignment, Lisa tells them what to expect next.

"We start practicing tomorrow," she says. "We'll have a read-through of your mission script, so all of you will be familiar with what you have to say and do. Later, we'll have our first hands-on practice in *Columbia*. But first it's time to tour the Rocket Park. You have to know how the space program got started if you want to be part of it now."

On their way to the Rocket Park, the trainees walk past *Pathfinder*, the only full-size model of the complete space shuttle in the United States. It towers ten stories above their heads. In the Rocket Park, Wyle team sees the finest collection of real rockets in the world. As they tour the exhibits, they learn about the evolution of rocketry, from the lethal German V-2 rockets of World War II, to intercontinental ballistic missiles, to the world's largest, most powerful rocket, *Saturn V.*

At last the campers reach *Saturn V.* This massive rocket, taller than a thirty-six-story building when the rocket stood on the launchpad, was designed to propel Apollo crews of astronauts to the moon. President John F. Kennedy wanted the United States to reach the

moon before 1970. NASA succeeded.

On July 20, 1969, Mission Commander Neil Armstrong set foot on the lunar surface. For two hours, he and Buzz Aldrin, commander of *Apollo 11*'s Lunar Module, took samples of soil and rock, set up experiments, and hopped like kangaroos in the powdery dust of the moon.

Space Camp's *Saturn V*, one of three remaining test vehicles of this mighty line of moon rockets, lies on the ground. Its three stages are pulled apart so that people can see its engines. Jessica is allowed to climb into a booster engine in order to show her teammates how big it is. Each of these five booster engines consumed 5,000 gallons of propellant a second to develop the 7.6 million pounds of thrust needed to hurl *Apollo* into space.

Inspired by the rockets they've seen and touched, the team members head back to Habitat to begin building two-stage model rockets of their own. It will take several work sessions before they are ready for launch on Wednesday.

The rockets are constructed from kits under the watchful eye of Lisa, who guides the trainees through the process. As they work, she emphasizes how important it is to do a good job. The Wyle team will be graded on how well its rockets perform. But that's not the main reason the members need to do their best.

Each rocket is designed to carry a "cricketnaut" in the clear plastic capsule at the top. The safety of every camper's cricket astronaut, if he or she chooses to launch one, depends on how well the rocket has been built!

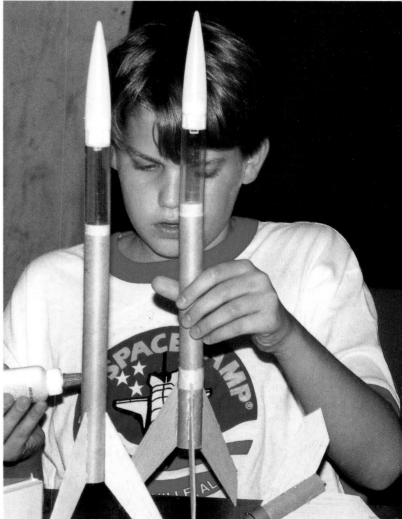

"My cricket will be fine," promises Reed. "I won't let him *or* the team down!"

That night the campers have a barbecue under *Pathfinder*. It is the centerpiece of Space Shuttle Park, and of the trainees' dreams.

"Man, that's where I'm going someday!" says Jonathan, sitting and eating his hamburger in *Pathfinder*'s huge shadow. "In a bird just like that one. I love it here! This is the best camp I've ever been to!"

"Me, too," says Jessica, licking barbecue sauce from her fingers.

After dinner, everyone enjoys the first of five movies about space exploration that they'll see in the Spacedome Theater—the IMAX film *Energy, Energy!*

The energy spills over into Wyle team's first night in the sleeping bays. Lights-out is 9:30 P.M. They're tired, but who can sleep?

In Sagittarius Bay, Wyle team members Jessica, Nikki, and Tasha Woodyard, from California, compare notes with their bunkmates. Is it possible they've been here only one day? They've learned and done so much already, it seems as if they have been here forever.

In Orion, the energy overload is enough to short out Space Camp. It takes all of night counselor Jay's skill to calm the boys. But the energy fizzles at last. By ten everyone is asleep. What was the first day like? Incredible! Fantastic! Exhausting...

DAY TWO
Astronaut Training

"Up and at 'em, Wyle! It's six o'clock!" says Jay.

"Oh, no!"

Oh, yes. By seven, Jay has his team out under *Pathfinder* for their wake-up exercise routine. An astronaut must be fit!

"Let's get some spirit here!" the trainer shouts. "Twenty-five jumping jacks! One! Two! Three! Four! Pick those feet up! Jump some more!"

By seven-thirty, everyone's chowing down breakfast in the cafeteria. Scrambled eggs. Bacon. French toast. Hot biscuits. Cereal. Juice and milk. Even picky eaters find something they like.

After breakfast, Astronaut Training

starts. Jay turns the Wyle team back to Lisa. She leads them to the Space Museum, where there are exhibits to see and hands-on training devices to work with.

They visit mock-ups for the Hubble Space Telescope, the Skylab space station, the Lunar Module, and the real *Apollo 16* capsule, which took three astronauts to the moon in 1972. They learn about the history of space-suit development, from the early rigid suits to the new flexible ones.

Tasha, Jessica, and fellow teammate Chris Rubery, from Texas, climb into Space Camp's replica of the Apollo Command Module Mission Simulator. The original module was once used to train astronauts to fly to the moon. Alan Shepard, America's first man in space, trained in a machine similar to this one.

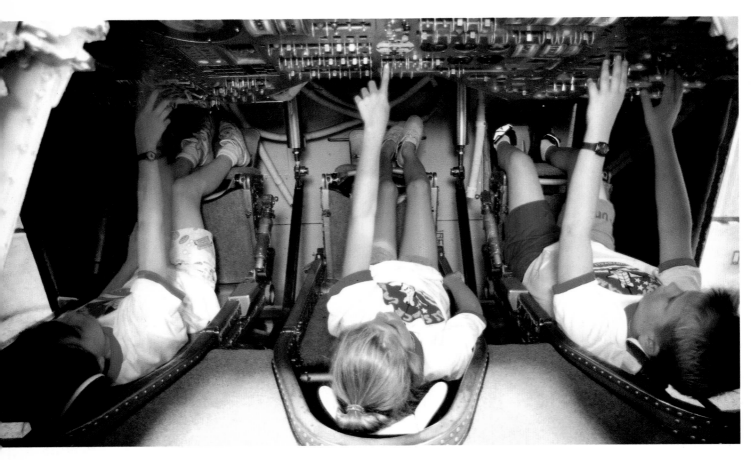

The Command Module was the control center for the Apollo spacecraft. It was where the three-man crew lived and worked the entire time the astronauts were in space. Missions lasted for up to twelve days. The only time the crew left the module was when the mission commander and Lunar Module commander went down to the moon's surface. Mission accomplished, they returned to Earth in this cramped vehicle.

Space Camp's module shows a portion of the compact cockpit. The ceiling is lined with brightly lit instrument panels and controls. Apollo astronauts learned how to guide their spacecraft during actual flight using instruments like these.

"How could they take lying down for so long?" Chris marvels, as he stretches out on one of the three narrow, horizontal couches beneath the top of the unit.

"Tough," says Tasha. "They were very tough."

"They wanted to be there," reminds Jessica, "more than they wanted to be comfortable. And they got to fly to the moon."

Reed runs in the Space Station Mobility Trainer. This device simulates weightlessness by allowing him to walk in a complete circle: forward, backward, and upside down. Handrails help him stay fixed in one position.

Next Wyle hits the Space Museum's Training Floor for more hands-on astronaut training.

Chris finds out what it is like to be one-sixth his actual weight in the 1/6th Gravity Chair, or Moonwalk Trainer. The chair is suspended from a spring in the ceiling that can be adjusted to equal the lower gravity of the moon. Seated in this chair, Chris is freed from the forces that normally pull him down on Earth. He jogs, glides from side to side, bounces like a tennis ball—in slow motion.

"This must be how Neil Armstrong felt when he walked on the moon. No wonder he didn't want to stop! I don't want to either," Chris cries.

Mission Specialist Eric tries the Five Degrees of Freedom Chair he'll be using during the flight. NASA used it to teach Gemini and Apollo trainees how to work in the microgravity, or weightlessness, of space during space walks. Strapped securely in his seat, his chair gliding on pressurized air like a Hovercraft, he is tossed five different ways by Lisa. Forward! Backward! Roll! Pitch! Yaw! This is how he would tumble in space

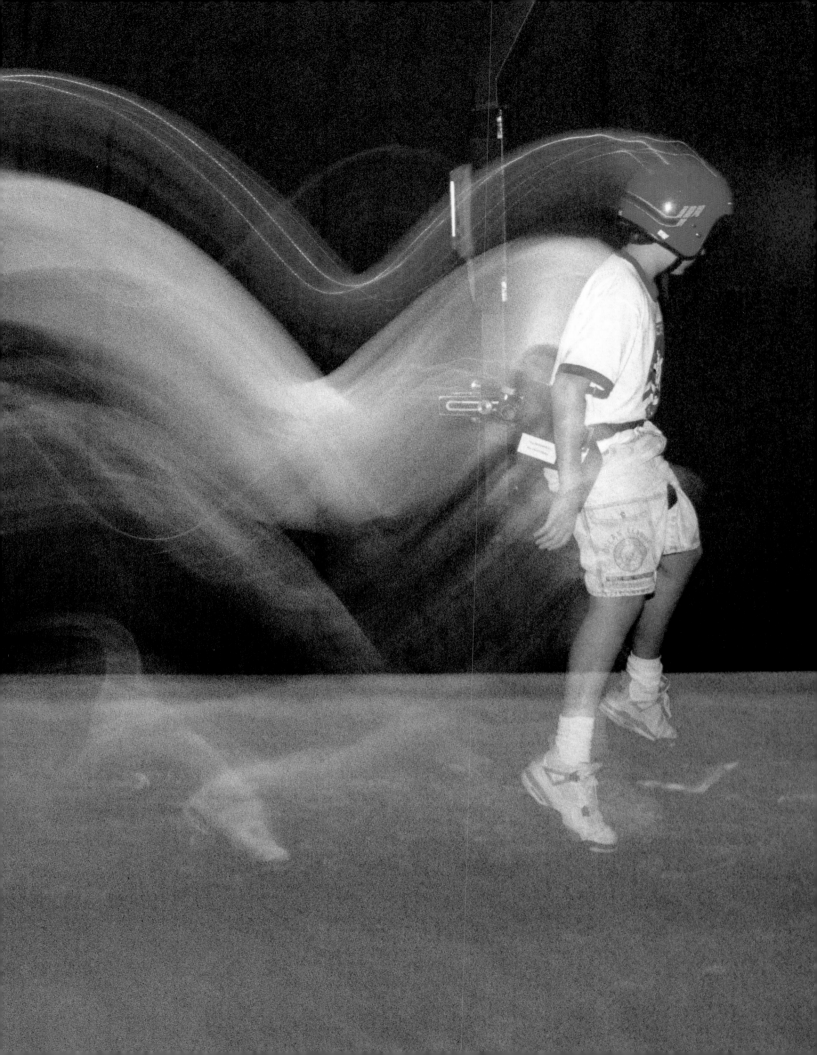

if he didn't anchor himself to a foothold or handhold in the cargo bay of his spacecraft.

Mission specialist Nikki prepares for her EVA in the Manned Maneuvering Unit, or MMU. This is a self-contained backpack unit. It was designed to allow astronauts to fly free in space without being tethered to the shuttle. Using this vehicle, astronauts can perform tasks, rescue a stranded astronaut, or visit another spacecraft.

Fitted out in a space suit, Nikki controls the movement of her MMU easily, using switches mounted in the arms of the unit. She can move in any direction, or rotate in a complete circle. In space, she could also move up and down.

"Great!" she cries. "I can't wait to do *this* again!"

The closest thing to a weightless experience on Earth is found underwater. Later in the week the Wyle team will go to the pool at the University of Alabama. There they'll get into bathing suits and do astronaut water training. They'll practice emergency exits from the orbiter, learn water survival techniques, build tetrahedrons underwater, and swim through hoops to simulate entering the spacecraft through an air lock.

Today they watch an older camper practice an EVA in the Underwater Astronaut Trainer (UAT), next to the Training Floor. The UAT is a huge tank filled with water. A mock-up of the outside of the orbiter lies at the bottom of the pool, so trainees, dressed in space suits, can practice repairing the craft in microgravity conditions. This is how real astronauts train.

Finally the team visits the gift shop. Cory buys Astronaut Ice Cream and shares it with his friends. Freeze-dried into chalklike lumps, the ice cream looks horrible. It is also so dry that you have to rush to a water fountain after eating it, to wet your tongue. But once it melts in your mouth, it tastes great.

Space meals have come a long way from the early tubes of food that astronauts squeezed out like toothpaste. The children learn that, on the space station, they can look forward to real ice cream!

□   □   □

That night, Jay persuades his team to settle down early. The next day is Tomorrow's Technology Day. How can they get ready for Tomorrow if they don't get some sleep tonight?

DAY THREE

Tomorrow's Technology

The Wyle team's leap into Tomorrow begins with a ride on the Space Camp bus. They rattle along the road to Marshall Space Flight Center, where they'll see a mock-up of *Freedom*, the proposed space station. Someday *Freedom* will allow people to live and work in space for up to six months at a time. For now it stands in a four-story hangarlike building at the Space Flight Center.

The space station is enormous. And the full-scale mock-up of its core modules, built by Boeing, is only part of it. When the campers enter it, they learn that these modules will be used for laboratories, living quarters, and work areas for the six to eight members of the crew.

The space shuttle will transport *Freedom* into orbit, piece by piece, some time late in the twentieth century. The station will be assembled in space by astronaut scientists and technicians, working with the help of the shuttle's robotic arm. Using *Freedom* as the first link, future astronauts could slowly build more and more space stations, reaching to the moon and beyond.

The team explores *Freedom*'s living quarters, or Habitation Module. Each crew member will have a living space of his or her own. The cubicles will have a sleeping bag, storage compartments, and a stereo headset. They may even have TV sets and VCRs.

Bathrooms will have toilets that vacuum out wastes. Showers will be tightly enclosed, so that water drops can't escape and float around the station in a permanent rainstorm.

Meals will be packaged so that food and liquids can't drift around the cabin in sticky globules. Meal packets will be prepared in the kitchen area and warmed in a microwave oven. Robotic arms and robots will do everyday chores. Astronaut energy will be saved for important work.

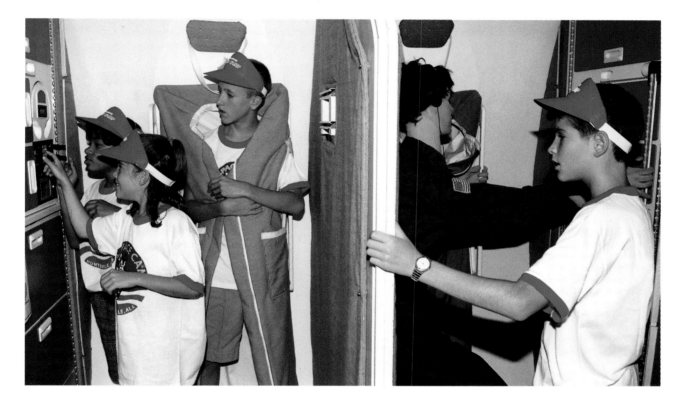

Jonathan Anderson climbs into one of the sleeping bags fastened to the wall. Since there's no up or down in space, it doesn't matter where you sleep. In the exercise facility, a dummy astronaut works out on the rowing machine. If you stay in space too long without exercising, your heart and muscles shrink and your bones get weak. You need to exercise about two hours in space to equal twenty minutes of exercise on Earth!

Excited by what they've seen, the team

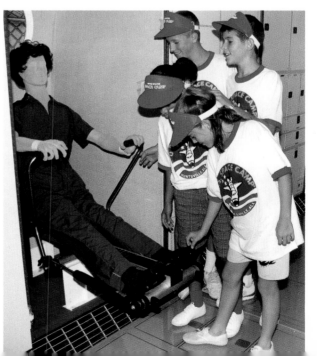

members return to Space Camp and head out for their own lunar mission. They'll perform this in Space Camp's lunar base in the Rocket Park.

As part of their study of the future, they've learned that NASA plans to send astronauts back to the moon in the first part of the twenty-first century. This time, astronauts will stay. First a temporary moon base will be built as a base for operations. A permanent moon colony will follow.

Wyle's mission today mimics that NASA mission of the future. It allows the campers to experience what the work of lunar-colony pioneers will be like.

Lisa divides them into four teams, each with a separate job to do. They ride to the lunar landing site in the camp's Lunar Buggy. All are dressed in Apollo-style space suits with life-support packs. These space suits are like one-man spacecraft, designed to protect the astronauts from the hostile environment of space. Without space suits on the moon, the astronauts' blood would soon begin to boil!

"I feel like I'm boiling right here in Huntsville," says Nikki, laughing. "Too bad these suits aren't air-conditioned, like they are for hot days on the moon."

Still, her Lunar Base Team wastes no time erecting a lightweight tent as a temporary moon base and shelter.

The Surveyor Team examines Space Camp's Surveyor. The real Surveyor is an unmanned probe landed on the moon in 1967 to map the lunar surface. The youngsters inspect the legs

of the lunar lander to see how it has fared after years of exposure to the weather on the moon.

The ALSEP Team (Apollo Lunar Surface Experiment Package) conducts tests to determine the heat on the surface of the crater. The Geological Team collects "moon rocks" and "lunar soil samples," just as real astronauts have done. Jessica helps her partner Cory describe and bag everything to take back to Earth for analysis.

As the Wyle team settles down that night, its members have plenty to think about. There seems to be no limit to the future. One day they may be living in space. Permanently. It's an awesome thought.

DAY FOUR

Rocket Launch Day

Rocket Launch Day! Jessica and Nikki walk to the launch site with the rest of the Wyle team. Now they'll find out whether the rockets they've built so carefully will fly or flop.

Lisa loads the rockets with the two rocket engines, each containing a pellet of solid fuel. The booster engine in the bottom stage launches the rocket. The one in the second stage deploys the parachute once the rocket is airborne. The parachute helps the rocket's capsule return safely to the ground.

A counselor arrives with a container of live crickets. Everyone has decided to launch a cricketnaut, which simulates a *real* astronaut. Jena gazes anxiously at hers. She believes she's built her rocket well, to keep the insect safe. She knows that bees and spiders have survived many space flights in space shuttle and Skylab experiments. But what about *her* cricket? Her rocket? For a moment she feels the agonizing sense of responsibility that NASA engineers must experience as the clock ticks off the seconds to a manned launch.

Jessica and Jonathan Brooks launch their rockets first. Bobby McKnight, from Florida, and Reed Barrickman are next. Their teammates, sheltering behind the protective baffle, shout the countdown. "*Five . . . four . . . three . . . two . . . one . . .* FIRE!"

The hiss of ignition is followed by a whoosh and a trail of smoke as a rocket races skyward, a thousand feet above the park. Then, *pop!* The candy-striped parachute bursts open, and the rocket, with its tiny passenger, floats to the ground.

When all the rockets have been launched, the children race to retrieve them. Every trip

into space has an element of danger. That's the price we pay to explore new worlds. The children know that. But still they run as fast as they can to find their capsules. Did the cricketnauts survive their flight? Most of them did. Tasha's cricket rests on her sleeve a moment before hopping into the long, cool grass. She wonders if it'll even remember the biggest hop it ever made.

That night, in bed, Jonathan Brooks dreams with his eyes wide open. Tonight the campers had seen the IMAX film *Hail Columbia!* Jonathan will never forget it.

Seated beneath the huge OMNIMAX screen, surrounded by soaring images and an explosive sound track, he felt he was *there* at the historic 1981 voyage of America's first space shuttle, *Columbia*—the very shuttle whose namesake he will command tomorrow in his Space Camp mission!

He remembers lift-off...the roar of *Columbia*'s solid rocket boosters thrusting the giant shuttle away from Earth...the shouts and tears of Mission Control at Kennedy Space Center. He can still hear the cries of hundreds of Space Campers: *"Go! Go! Go!"*

Up there, *that's* where he wants to go! He knows it more surely now than ever. Today the crickets flew. Tonight he saw *Columbia* fly. Tomorrow it's his turn.

It's only Space Camp's *Columbia*, of course, not NASA's. But it's a start. He's on his way. . . .

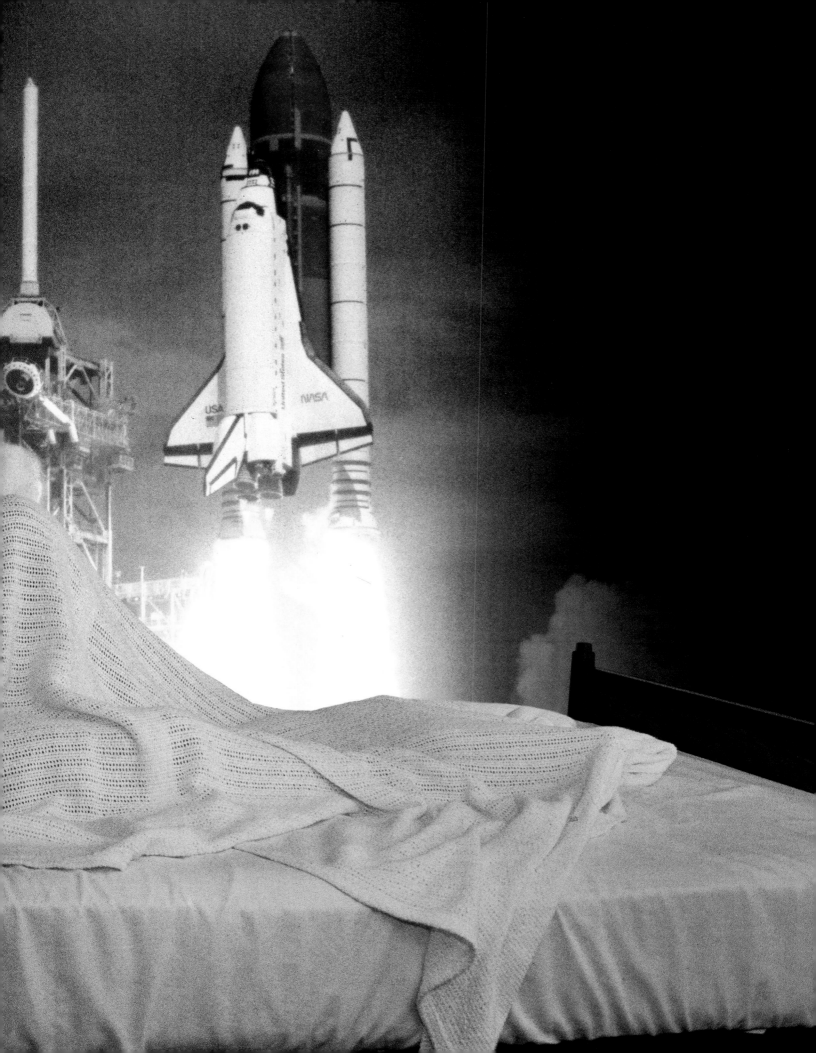

DAY FIVE
Mission Day

For the first time, Wyle team members dress in their NASA-style flight suits. They look like real astronauts. But they don't feel it. They wonder if they're ready.

"Of *course* you're ready!" says Lisa. "You've worked hard all week, learned a lot. You've read through the mission script over and over again, practiced your jobs. You know them. The important thing is, you've become a *team*. I'm proud of you!"

"What about the malfunctions?" asks Jonathan Brooks.

He, as commander, and Jonathan Anderson, as flight director, will have to solve two in-flight emergencies. These malfunctions aren't in the mission script. They're added to see how the children deal with a crisis. Every mission has different "emergencies," just as real shuttle missions do. And like real NASA commanders, the two Jonathans will have to solve the problems themselves, using what they've learned in their week at Space Camp.

"You'll know what to do when it happens," promises Lisa. "I trust you."

All right! The team divides into ground and flight crews. Jonathan Brooks and his team enter *Columbia* through the air lock and strap themselves into their seats.

Jonathan Anderson and his squad take their positions at Mission Control. They clamp on their headsets. Seated in front of the monitors that will show *Columbia*'s position and technical status at all times, they prepare to lead the flight crew through the carefully scripted steps toward lift-off.

The mission program is punched in on *Columbia*'s computers, and the monitor screens spring to life. In *Columbia*'s cockpit, the monitor is like a TV screen. It shows full-color images of a real NASA shuttle launch, orbit, and reentry. To Jonathan and Jessica, strapped into their seats in front of this monitor, it feels as if they are watching their mission unfold as it happens. Their eyes are riveted to the picture of the shuttle poised on the launchpad. For them it has become *their* shuttle, ready to leap into space.

Earphones crackle as communication between orbiter and Mission Control begins. A sound track starts, filling the orbiter and the earphones of the Mission Control team with the sounds of an authentic NASA mission.

Tasha, launch and landing director, gulps. Her stomach gives one lurch, then settles as she speaks the first line from her mission script:

We are just a few seconds away from resuming the countdown for Space Transportation System-35. *Columbia*'s crew has completed final preflight checks and is ready for lift-off.

Once countdown begins, the mission runs like clockwork. Precise times for each line, each action, are listed on the left of the page in the mission script. The passing minutes and seconds flash on the TV monitors.

For the hour the mission takes, Wyle team members truly believe that the adventure is real. They act as if their very lives depend on how well they perform.

In the cockpit of *Columbia*, Jonathan and Jessica are calm but serious. Jessica advises Mission Control that "all systems are ready and we are go for launch."

T–0:10   LAUNCH/LANDING DIRECTOR TASHA: T-minus 10 seconds...8, 7. Main engine start. 3, 2, 1, booster ignition.

An ominous rumble, like a volcano about to erupt, electrifies the team as *Columbia*'s solid rocket boosters ignite, generating a thrust of over five million pounds. Eight explosive charges snap the bolts that hold the shuttle to its pad. The rumbling becomes a roar.

T–0:00   LAUNCH/LANDING DIRECTOR TASHA: Lift-off.

T+0:01   COMMANDER JONATHAN BROOKS: Roger, lift-off.

It's impossible to miss. The roar of the shuttle bursting free is heard outside on the Training Floor. Inside, the volcanic thunder of the engines floods the cabin like molten lava. An avalanche of sound hits the crew, pinning them to their seats.

Chairs vibrate. Floors shake. In the cockpit, the monitor screen shows *Columbia* hurtling into space, riding a tail of orange flame. In mid-deck, you don't need a monitor. The shock of lift-off registers in Cory's eyes.

The noise continues as *Columbia* streaks skyward. The crew watches as the solid rocket boosters separate, their job of launch accomplished. They float down to the ocean on parachutes. The ride is smoother now.

At fifty-eight miles above Earth, Jessica throttles down *Columbia*'s mighty engines, then cuts them off. The huge external tank, its fuel exhausted by the hard climb, separates and falls away. Jessica and Jonathan Brooks watch it burning up in the atmosphere as it plummets toward the ocean.

Then Jessica shuts down the auxiliary power units and maneuvers the shuttle into proper position. An unearthly silence fills the spacecraft. They're in orbit!

No time to celebrate. There's work to be done. Mission Control gives a new order.

> 10:00 FLIGHT DIRECTOR JONATHAN ANDERSON: *Columbia*, you are go for EVA and payload operations.

Eric and Nikki, the mission specialists, suit up and crawl out through the air lock to perform the EVAs they have practiced during the week. Seated in the MMU, Nikki changes a solar panel. Balancing in the temperamental 5DF Chair, Eric connects a hose from a reserve hydrogen fuel tank to a supply tank to replenish the shuttle's store of fuel. EVAs completed, they return to the orbiter, remove their space suits, and strap themselves back into their seats.

At the same time, Cory and John, payload specialists, perform scientific experiments in mid-deck. They are assisted by Reed and Chris, the two science specialists on the ground. They activate solar telescopes to get superclear pictures of the surface of the sun. Another experiment is to make rubber balls so small they can be seen only by microscope.

When all experiments and EVAs have been completed, it's time for *Columbia* to come home.

> 27:00 COMMANDER JONATHAN BROOKS: This is the commander. We are ready to start entry preparations. All crew members will return to their seats.

Suddenly it happens. Flight director Jonathan is warned that a violent storm has blown up over Kennedy Space Center. *Columbia* is scheduled to land there. What will they do now?

Commander Jonathan stays cool. They have studied this kind of emergency, and he knows there is always another place to go. From the four alternatives flashed on his monitor screen, he chooses Edwards Air Force Base in California. They alter course and continue procedures to bring the shuttle back to Earth.

Then a red warning light flashes on Jonathan Anderson's screen in Mission Control. It alerts him to a fuel leak in one of the engines that allows the orbiter to maneuver. *Columbia* could blow up in the heat of reentry or lose the ability to turn properly!

Jonathan relays the bad news to the shuttle's commander. Jonathan Brooks and Jessica exchange glances. What to do? Jonathan doesn't remember studying this particular problem. Then he recalls something he read in a book about space. In an emergency, the important

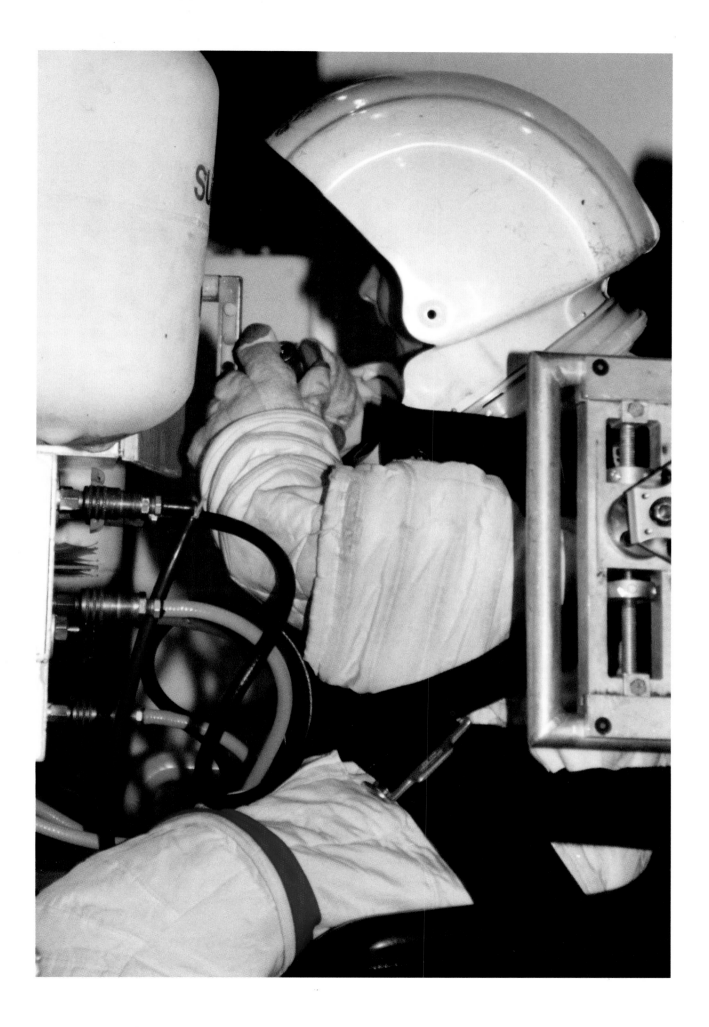

thing is to *think*. Choose the course of action that offers the best chance of survival for your crew. Then act.

He considers the options that pop up on his monitor screen: abort the mission, cancel experiments to save fuel, wait for a rescue shuttle, or shut down the bad engine and get by with the remaining fuel.

Jonathan doesn't hesitate. He shuts off the leaky engine and trusts to his judgment, his skill, and Wyle teamwork to bring them safely home. There's enough fuel left in the tanks, he believes, to complete their mission.

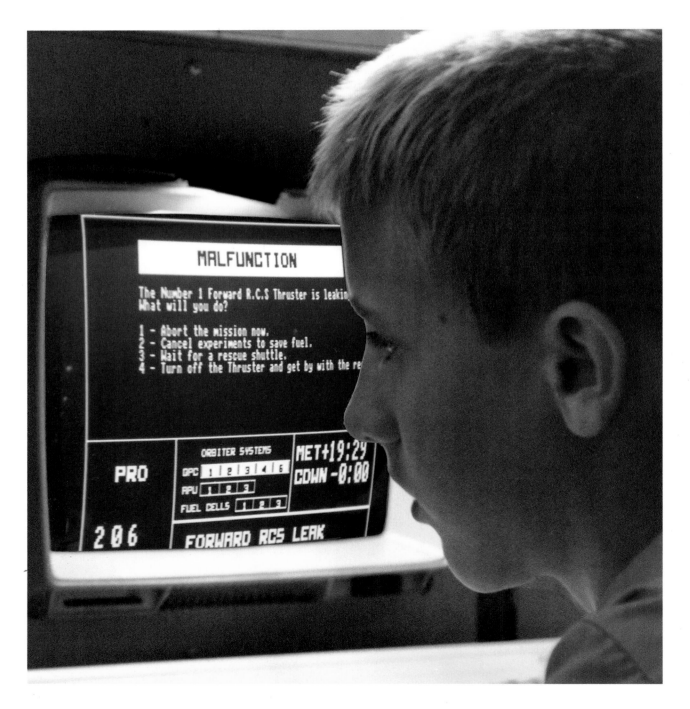

He's right! Jonathan and Jessica fly the orbiter in, using their instruments. They land smoothly, like a plane, supported by their teammates on Mission Control.

48:40   LAUNCH/LANDING DIRECTOR TASHA: Shuttle at 200 feet.

49:00   PILOT JESSICA: (Presses landing gear arm.) Landing gear armed.

            LAUNCH/LANDING DIRECTOR TASHA: 95 feet.

49:10   PILOT JESSICA: (Presses landing gear down.) Gear down.

49:20   LAUNCH/LANDING DIRECTOR TASHA: 10 feet…5, 4, 3, 2, 1.

49:25   COMMANDER JONATHAN BROOKS: (Screen shows "WOW!") Touchdown.

50:00   COMMANDER JONATHAN BROOKS: (Screen shows "Wheel Stop.") Houston, *Columbia.* We're home.

            FLIGHT DIRECTOR JONATHAN ANDERSON: Welcome home and congratulations on a job well done.

"Wyle! Wyle! Wyle!"

The team goes wild. They come together in an explosion of energy, like twelve solid rocket boosters. But who needs an orbiter? They're still in orbit! And they don't want to come down.

Lisa runs over and hugs everybody. "Good job, Wyle! I was worried about that leak. But you handled it just right. I'm proud of you. Really proud."

"I wish I could do it again," says Jonathan Brooks. "It was the best moment of my life."

DAY SIX
Graduation and Good-bye

Graduation is early. Everyone gets up at five-thirty to finish packing and cleaning up. They can't believe it's over. How can they break up the team? Just when they got together!

Colonel Mike Mullane, a pilot and mission specialist who flew shuttle missions in 1984 and 1988, is the graduation speaker. Jonathan Brooks is excited to hear him. Colonel Mullane was one of the Discovery astronauts in the IMAX movie he saw, *The Dream Is Alive.*

Colonel Mullane encourages the eager campers to cling to the dreams that brought them to Space Camp. "If a kid from Albuquerque, New Mexico, like me, can do it," he assures them, "you can, too. Take lots of math and science in school. Study hard. Get good grades. Go to college. Take things that NASA can use, like engineering or science. If you do, someday you can go even farther than I did. I've orbited Earth, lived and worked in space. But *you*... one of you out there can become one of the first astronauts to live and work on the moon. One of you might even plant the American flag on Mars!"

Jonathan swallows hard, wondering if he will be that astronaut.

"You'll make it, if you want it bad enough," the colonel finishes, and sits down.

The audience claps wildly, and Jonathan makes a fierce, silent promise to himself and to the astronaut he admires. "I'll make it. Watch for me!"

Then, team by team, the campers are called up to the podium and presented with their graduation certificates and silver Space Camp wings.

Jonathan Brooks's name is called. As he walks up proudly to get his wings, he can't help remembering what he told Lisa on Day One, before he knew what being an astronaut was all about. "I'd dive into a pool of steaming poison on Pluto to be an astronaut," he asserted, "or fly up close to the sun if they told me to!"

Lisa didn't seem impressed by his courage. "Nobody would order you to do something they knew would hurt you," she said. "And nobody wants to go into space with a daredevil. *Real* astronauts have discipline, education, training. They care about their mission and their teammates. It's not like the movies, you know."

Well, he learned a lot since he made those boasts. And he's going to keep on learning, too, at Space Camp's Academy I next summer. Later, college. Perhaps the Air Force Academy.

He'll keep his grades up. It's not so hard, when you're shooting for something really important. . . .

"Congratulations, Jonathan," says Director Edward Buckbee, shaking his hand. "I hear you did a great job!"

"Thanks," says Jonathan. He pins on his wings and admires his certificate. He's going to frame it when he gets back to Texas.

Once the ceremony is over, campers disperse quickly. Cars pull out of parking lots; buses head off to the airport. Soon only Bobby, Tasha, Chris, and Jessica are left of the Wyle team. Sitting together, waiting for their bus, they think about going home.

"I've changed," says Tasha, thoughtfully. "I wonder if anyone will notice. . . ."

Shy Tasha hasn't decided, as Jonathan has, to seek a career in the space program. But she's

learned she can be a leader and do an important job well. Like other members of the Wyle team, she'll take that new confidence in herself back home with her.

The other Wyle team members know they have changed, too. They've grown as they've learned to make new friends, operate computers, build and launch rockets, fly a successful Space Camp mission.

The biggest difference, however, is that they view their future with new eyes. They've seen images of stars, planets, and galaxies beyond the planet where they live. They've taken an imaginary flight in the kind of shuttle that may allow them to visit those places one day. They've toured a model of the future space station, where they, or their children, may actually live. Their world has expanded to include the possibility of the universe.

The four campers look at their parting gift from Space Camp: the team address list. They don't have to lose touch!

When their bus is announced, they pick up their bags and move out. Tomorrow Space Camp will be quiet. But on Sunday a new training week begins. Another group of children will pour into Habitat. Another group will be Wyle team.

"You coming back next year?" asks Tasha.

"No," says Chris, who wants to be a newspaperman. "But I won't forget you. Maybe someday I'll write about one of us going into space."

"Great!" says Jessica. "Maybe it'll be me. I'm coming back here next year to keep learning."

"Me, too," says Bobby. "See you then!"